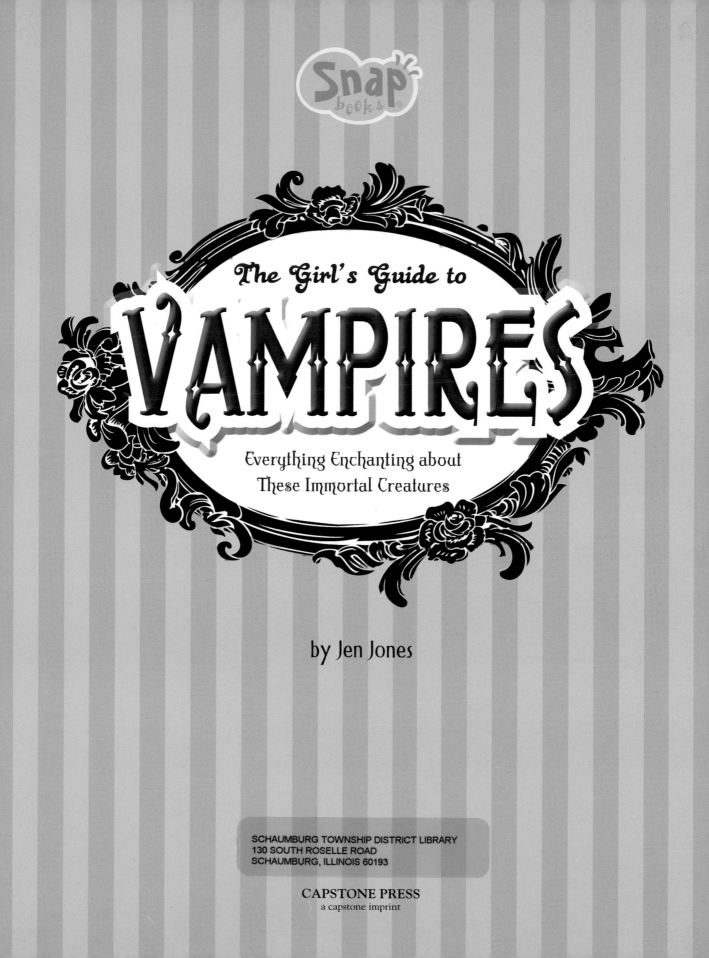

The Girl's Guide to VAMPIRES

Everything Enchanting about
These Immortal Creatures

by Jen Jones

CAPSTONE PRESS
a capstone imprint

Snap Books are published by Capstone Press,
151 Good Counsel Drive, P.O. Box 669, Mankato, Minnesota 56002.
www.capstonepub.com

Books published by Capstone Press are manufactured with paper
containing at least 10 percent post-consumer waste.

Library of Congress Cataloging-in-Publication Data
Jones, Jen.
 The girl's guide to vampires : everything enchanting about these immortal creatures / by Jen Jones.
     p. cm. — (Snap Books. Girls' guides to everything unexplained)
 Includes bibliographical references and index.
 Summary: "Describes the mystery, cool characteristics, and allure of vampires, including historical and
contemporary examples"—Provided by publisher.
 ISBN 978-1-4296-5452-4 (library binding)
 1. Vampires—Juvenile literature. I. Title. II. Series.
 BF1556.J66 2011
 398'.45—dc22   2010025211

Editorial Credits
Editor: Kathryn Clay
Designer: Tracy Davies
Media Researcher: Marcie Spence
Production Specialist: Laura Manthe

Printed in the United States of America in North Mankato, Minnesota.

072011
006241R

Contents

Chapter One

Dive into the Dark Side

Long ago, vampires were mostly known as scary, blood-sucking Dracula types. But thanks to hits like the Twilight series and *The Vampire Diaries*, vampires are quickly becoming swoon-worthy superstars.

So are vampires charming heartthrobs or evil undead?

It all depends on the vampire! Creatures of the night, vampires are full of wow-worthy powers and mysterious ways. It's no wonder they've become a pop-culture sensation.

Twilight

The Vampire Diaries

All vampires are **immortal**. They live forever by drinking human and animal blood. But the path to becoming a vampire can vary. Some people rise as vampires after they die. Others become vampires after being bitten by one. In the Twilight series, some characters are turned into vampires to keep them alive.

 Vampires can also be born.

In the past, people thought they could spot vampire babies. In some countries, babies born with teeth or red hair were suspected of being vampires.

Cute baby or evil vampire?

immortal: able to live forever

But knowing all this, one question remains. Are vampires real? Some people say that vampires are made-up characters. Yet history shows that people believed in blood-drinking demons and witches even in ancient times. The jury may be out on whether vampires are fact or fiction. But you can decide for yourself. Take a fang-filled flip through these pages to find out what vampires are all about.

Coffins are home to the evil undead.

Chapter Two

A Walk Down Vampire Lane

Because vampires can live forever, it's no surprise that they've been around for centuries. It was once commonly believed that **corpses** rose from the grave to drink human blood. Doing this would allow living corpses to live among humans. Different cultures added their own twists on the vampire myth. In Russia, people believed that vampires were former witches. Greeks believed people risked becoming the undead if they weren't buried in ground that had been blessed.

Romanians once believed that doomed souls rose from the grave. They called these vampire-like beings *strigoi*. To Romanians, there were many ways to seal your fate as a vampire. Being buried face-up or dying without getting married were ways to become a vampire.

Many people think Romania is the home of vampires. In fact, Romania once claimed its ruler was a vampire. Vlad III, the Impaler, ruled the area of Wallachia in the mid-1400s. His nasty practice of killing his enemies made him the inspiration for the popular vampire Dracula.

Vlad III, the Impaler

While people were deathly afraid of vampires centuries ago, that's no longer the case. Fast-forward to today, when vampires stare at us from giant movie billboards. Thanks to the Twilight books and movies, some people even dream of marrying an Edward Cullen-style vamp! It's a whole new world where vampires are welcomed with open arms.

FACT

Vlad III, the Impaler's last name was Dracul.

corpse: a dead body

READ, WATCH and LEARN

Want to be able to pass any vampire quiz? First you'll need to do some required (but totally fun) research. Check out these stories you can really sink your teeth into.

READ IT: *Vampire Island* by Adele Griffin

Lexie, Maddy, and Hudson are part vegetarian vampires and part fruit bats. They are on a mission to rid Manhattan of evil blood-sucking vampires. On top of saving the planet, the trio faces normal stuff like fitting in at school. Plus, they also have to deal with not-so-normal stuff like hiding their powers from classmates.

READ IT: *My Sister the Vampire* by Sienna Mercer

This four-book series is like a vampire version of *The Parent Trap*. When Olivia transfers to a new school, she's shocked to meet her long-lost twin sister, Ivy. As Olivia gets to know Ivy, she finds out that they're not entirely alike. Ivy just happens to be a vampire! Now it's Olivia's job to keep Ivy's secret.

WATCH IT: *Twilight* (series)

Based on the Stephenie Meyer book series, the Twilight movies have collected millions of dollars and hearts! The story follows the mysterious vampires and werewolves that haunt a quiet Washington town. After Bella discovers the town's secrets, her life is never the same.

WATCH IT: *Buffy the Vampire Slayer*

Based on a 1992 flick of the same name, this TV series is widely considered a classic. *Buffy the Vampire Slayer* shares the adventures of Buffy and "The Scooby Gang." This group of friends band together to fight evil. The show also follows Buffy's drama-filled love life. After all, it's hard to slay vampires if you fall for them! Though the show isn't on TV anymore, fans continue to enjoy the story through comic books and DVDs.

VAMPIRE STORIES

Vampire stories have been around for hundreds of years. But it wasn't until the 1800s that vampires started to show up on the page. The first work of vampire fiction was the 1819 short story "The Vampyre." Next came Bram Stoker's *Dracula* in 1897. This best-seller became the basis for future vampire stories and a must-read for vampire lovers.

These two stories cleared the way for silent films like 1913's *The Vampire* and 1922's *Nosferatu*. *Nosferatu* was based on the story of Count Dracula. It was the first flick to show a vampire squirm in sunlight! It also started a trend. Six movies made in the 1930s and 1940s starred a Dracula character. The best known film was 1931's *Dracula* with Bela Lugosi.

Bram Stoker's *Dracula*

Nosferatu

Bela Lugosi as Dracula

FACT

Nosferatu may be one form of the Romanian word for vampire.

While most classic flicks show vampires as evil villains, vampires have improved their status in recent years. Depending on the story, vampires may be shown as clever, mysterious, charming, or even lovable. The vampires on TV's *Buffy the Vampire Slayer* were great examples. Spike was a mischievous, sharp-tongued vampire, while Angel was a good-hearted romantic. Of course, just because vampires now show their lighter side doesn't mean they gave up on the darkness. In the *Twilight* series, the Cullen family must fight off their vampire urges when Bella is around.

Spike

Angel

One thing is for sure—vampires are more popular than ever. And they seem fine with all the attention.

The Cullen Family

Just because vampires don't like sunlight doesn't mean they can't be in the spotlight!

Chapter Three
Fang-Tastic Features

Movies and books have largely shaped how we picture vampires. And what a big picture it is! From Goth girls and spiky-haired punks to charming gentlemen, vampires have many looks. Yet from the classic Dracula to the Cullens, telltale signs give away any vampire. Keep an eye out for these features the next time you go out vampire-spotting!

Vampires thrive in darkness.

Pale skin: Why do most vampires look like the blood has drained from their faces? Because it has! The undead may have lots of special skills, but rocking a tan isn't one of them. Their pale skin is often cold to the touch.

Rosy lips: Lots of vampires have lips that are blood red. Maybe they're just cold, or maybe these vampires just finished snacking.

Mysterious eyes: Whether black, red, or gold in color, a vampire's eyes are almost always watchful. Many vampires also have super-large pupils. The oversized pupils make it easier to see at night.

Long fingernails: It may look like some vampires are in serious need of a manicure. Yet their sharp nails are great for snatching victims. In some tales, a vampire's fingernails also have a glassy, see-through look.

Dark hair: Not all vampires are brunettes, but most seem to be. Brothers Damon and Stefan from *The Vampire Diaries* are perfect examples. Their dark hair helps them blend into the night.

Fangs: What's a vampire without a few fangs? Thanks to these animal-like fangs, vampires can really sink their teeth into their victims.

None of these features are one size fits all. But if you spot several of them together, you just might be staring down a vampire!

VAMP IT UP

Vampires usually have dark, mysterious personalities and the style to match. Some vampires prefer classic Victorian looks, while others go for the heavy goth approach. Many vampires like to fade into the background with standard black from head to toe. No matter what look vampires choose, you can bet they keep these key items in their closets.

Some vampires rock the classic goth look.

Capes: No vampire's wardrobe is complete without a cape. The long silk or velvet cape with a red lining was made popular by Dracula. While many modern vampires favor a less formal look, they often wear capes at underground gatherings.

Dark clothes: It's unlikely you'll find much variety in this wardrobe. For vampires, black is standard. No bright colors for these dark dressers. Just watch *The Vampire Diaries* for proof. The characters on this show are often dimly dressed.

Sunglasses: Sunlight-sensitive vampires need all the tools they can get to keep the light out. If they must go out during the day, you can bet they'll have shades on.

Coffin: While a coffin may not fit in a closet, vampires keep them close by. For vampires, coffins symbolize coming back from the dead. Some vampires even sleep inside these peaceful, dark boxes.

QUIZ: Could Your Crush Be a Vampire?

Now that you know the signs of a vampire, find out if your crush is a real bloodsucker! This handy quiz will let you know if he fits the profile.

When it comes to sports, your crush is best at:

a) wrestling—it's mind-blowing how much weight he can lift.

b) basketball—his slam dunk is really something.

c) golf—he's definitely in the swing of things.

d) track and field—he can run like the wind!

What can your crush do that no else can?

a) He often knows exactly what I'm thinking.

b) He can see perfectly in the dark.

c) His math skills are amazing.

d) He's got super-tuned ears—he always hears me whispering to my BFF.

It's time to cuddle up with a DVD. Your crush requests:

a) *Dracula*

b) *Buffy the Vampire Slayer*

c) *High School Musical 3: Senior Year*

d) *Twilight: New Moon*

In history class, your crush is most fascinated by:

a) the Revolutionary War—he claims he was there!

b) tales of Old Europe

c) Lewis and Clark's expedition

d) the Salem witch trials

You sneak a peek into your crush's closet. What do you find?

a) Black is back! All of his clothes seem to be on the dark side.

b) several pairs of dark sunglasses

c) his favorite basketball jersey

d) a pair of industrial-strength nail clippers

You go out to dinner with your crush. What does he pick to eat?

a) He doesn't eat anything—he says he'll eat later.

b) a nice, juicy steak

c) spaghetti and meatballs with extra garlic toast

d) a side of beef—medium-rare

Look through your answers and see which vampire holds the keys to your heart! If you circled:

Mostly As: It's love at first bite! Your crush certainly sounds like a vampire.

Mostly Bs: Your crush has definite blood-sucking potential.

Mostly Cs: No pale prince for you—your crush is all human.

Mostly Ds: Your crush is no vampire—but he just might be a werewolf!

✛ ✛ ✛ ✛ ✛ ✛ ✛ ✛ ✛ ✛ ✛ ✛ ✛ ✛ ✛ ✛ ✛

Chapter Four

Out for Blood

Vampire Strengths

With vampires walking among us, it's wise to be aware of what they can do. It's useful info whether you're crushing on one or simply trying to steer clear. After all, vampires may look like humans, but they still have superhuman abilities! Among their most impressive skills is strength. In *Twilight*, Edward saves Bella from a crashing car. Fantastic moves like that are just everyday events in the life of a vampire. Here are a few more **supernatural** vampire powers:

Edward's strength carries Bella.

Sports skills: Vampires are awesome athletes. Like Superman, they have the ability to fly or leap tall buildings. Dracula could even scale walls like Spiderman. Some vampires move so fast that you might miss your chance to spot one.

Command of nature: Ever wish you could control the weather? Van Helsing, the vampire hunter in *Dracula*, discovered that vampires could make lightning. Vampires can also turn into animals such as bats and wolves.

Mind tricks: Vampires can perform all sorts of cool mind tricks. In the Twilight series, Alice can see the future. Edward can read minds. In the *Vampire* Marvel comics, some vampires can control thoughts by staring into someone's eyes.

Anti-aging: Who wouldn't want to be forever young? Vampires have the fountain of youth at their fang tips. Once they turn into vampires, they stay the same age forever.

Super-sharp senses: Imagine that all of your senses are on a dial, and a regular human is set to "one." Vampires can turn that dial up to 10! Night vision, sharp hearing, and a strong sense of smell are all vampire strengths.

supernatural: something that cannot be given an ordinary explanation

Vampire Weaknesses

Not all vampires are gentlemen heartthrobs like Edward Cullen. In fact, some of them are downright devilish! And since they're so powerful, it's a must to know some key survival skills. Here are some things you can use to fend off the fangs.

Garlic: In Bram Stoker's *Dracula*, the characters rub garlic around the house. Some people even wear garlic necklaces. In the past, garlic was stuffed into the mouths of dead people thought to be vampires. They believed that garlic's odor bothered the vampires' sense of smell. Others thought that because garlic keeps mosquitoes away, it must scare off other bloodsuckers too.

Religious items: In the battle of good versus evil, good always wins thanks to these religious items. Vampires find it difficult to harm people wearing crosses. Holy water blessed by church leaders can be thrown at attacking vampires. The water can also be sprinkled on their graves.

Sunlight: Want to make a vampire vanish? Let in some light! Though not all vampires hide out during the daytime, sunlight can seriously weaken their powers. In some cases, the light can even burn a vampire to death.

Loss of life force: If you lock up a vampire away from everything, it just might lose its monster powers. Vampires need to stick to a feeding schedule to survive—and therefore need access to animals and humans. Lack of food can mean a rapid loss of powers.

HOW TO SLAY A VAMPIRE

Slaying a vampire isn't easy, but someone has to do it!

Many believe the only way to kill a vampire is to drive a sharp stake through its heart.

Yet others say that the stake is just the first part. Cutting off the vampire's head or burning the body comes next. It's also important to bury the vampire's ashes or parts in different places. That way, the body can't come together again. And the same goes for the stake. Don't remove it, or the vampire could come back!

When it comes to vampires, there is certainly no shortage of legends. Their rich history and air of mystery make for endless interest! Whether you're a vampire slayer or a vampire groupie, dealing with vampires is always a blood-curdling ride.

Vampire killing kit

A wooden stake is one way to kill a vampire.

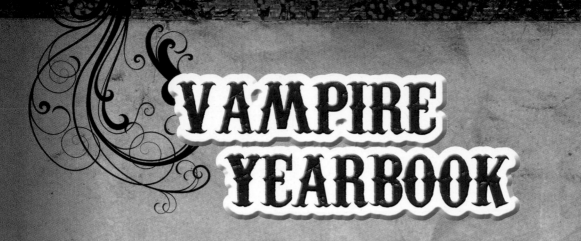

VAMPIRE YEARBOOK

Most Lucky in Love
Elena (*The Vampire Diaries*)

She's got two of the hottest vamps on TV fighting over her. Elena is a clear winner in this category!

Cutest Couple
Edward Cullen and Bella Swan (*Twilight*)

This couple's romance may be a roller coaster, but we can't get enough of the ride.

Most Mischievous
Four~Legged Friend
Bunnicula (*Bunnicula*)

Who says picture books
are just for little kids? This pet
bunny has got all the makings
of a vampire and a great story.

Biggest Dose of
Girl Power
**Buffy Summers
(*Buffy the Vampire Slayer*)**

Brave and strong, Buffy
could take any vampire or evil
creature that came her way.

Most Likely to Take You
Under Her Wing
Alice Cullen (Twilight)

Bella's just a bit out of her
comfort zone. Luckily she has
Alice to keep her away from
possible danger.

Most Unstoppable Sibs
**Olivia and Ivy
(*My Sister the Vampire*)**

Mess with this twosome and
you're in for double the trouble.

GLOSSARY

coffin (KAWF-in)—a long container into which a dead person is placed for burial

corpse (KORPS)—a dead body

culture (KUHL-chuhr)—the way of life, beliefs, and traditions of a group of people

demon (DEE-muhn)—a devil or an evil spirit

immortal (i-MOR-tuhl)—able to live forever

myth (MITH)—a story told by people in ancient times; myths often tried to explain natural events

pupil (PYOO-puhl)—the round, dark center of your eye that lets in light

supernatural (soo-pur-NACH-ur-uhl)—something that cannot be given an ordinary explanation

vegetarian (vej-uh-TER-ee-uhn)—someone who does not eat meat

READ MORE

Regan, Sally. *The Vampire Book: The Legends, The Lore, The Allure.* New York: Dorling Kindersley Limited, 2009.

Guillain, Charlotte. *Vampires.* Mythical Creatures. Chicago: Raintree, 2011.

Marx, Mandy R. *Great Vampire Legends.* Vampires. Mankato, Minn.: Capstone Press, 2011.

INTERNET SITES

FactHound offers a safe, fun way to find Internet sites related to this book. All of the sites on FactHound have been researched by our staff.

Here's all you do:

Visit *www.facthound.com*

Type in this code: 9781429654524

Super-cool stuff! Check out projects, games and lots more at
www.capstonekids.com

INDEX